SPECTRUM

Writing

Grade 2

Spectrum

An imprint of Carson-Dellosa Publishing LLC
Greensboro, North Carolina

Spectrum
An imprint of Carson-Dellosa Publishing LLC
P.O. Box 35665
Greensboro, NC 27425 USA

ISBN 0-7696-5282-4

7 8 9 10 11 WCR 15 14 13 12 11

053118454

Table of Contents Grade 2

Chapter 1 Writing Titles and Sentences

Chapter 2 Telling and Asking

Chapter 3 Telling How

Table of Contents, continued

Chapter 4 Describing

Chapter 5 Writing Stories

Chapter 1

Lesson 1 Write a Title

What is each picture about? Circle the best title. A title is a group of words that describe what a picture or story is about. The first and last words in a title are always capitalized. Important words in the title are also capitalized.

1. Fire Danger

   A Sunny Day

   Carl's House

2. Too Much Traffic

   Birds Fly South

   Back to School

3. Circus in Town

   Bike Safety

   Dancing Dogs

Lesson 1 Write a Title

Write a title with one or two words to tell what each picture is about.

1. The robot has claws.

2. The flowers are beautiful.

3. The fish lives in the ocean.

Tip	Remember, in a title, the first and last words are always capitalized. All important words are also capitalized.

Lesson 2 | Name That Story

The title of a story tells what the story is about. Read each story. Then, answer the question.

Holly is quiet all day. She won't talk or sing. She eats her food. She cleans her feathers. She seems to be waiting for something. What could it be? When Anna and Kenny get home, then we know. Holly says, "Where have you been? Where have you been?" Anna and Kenny laugh. Holly has been waiting for them all day.

1. What is the best title for this story? Circle your choice.

Anna and Kenny at School   Caring for a Parrot   Holly's Day

J.T. grinned all the way to school. He looked funny, but that was okay. Today was Mix-Up Day. His shoes didn't match. His wild pants did not match his striped shirt. Just to make sure, his shirt was on backward. When J.T. got to school, he saw a poster. It said, "Don't forget—Tomorrow is Mix-Up Day." J.T. stopped grinning.

2. What is the best title for this story? Circle your choice.

Mix-Up Day   J.T.'s Shirt   Signs at School

Lesson 2 Name That Story

Read the stories on this page. Then, read the titles in
the box. Choose the best title for each story. Write
the title on the line above the story. Remember to
leave a space between each word.

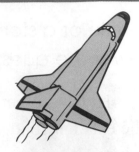

Happy Landing	A Ride in Space	Rocket Launch
Space Race	Moon Monster	No One at Home

_____

   The spaceship sailed through the sky. As Dale got close to the moon, he saw
a strange sight. Another spaceship sat in his landing spot. Dale looked at his
computer screen. The message said, "I win." Dale shook his head. His sister had
beaten him to the moon again.

_____

   Jan was looking forward to a good meal at the space station. It was almost
time to land. She looked at her screen, then she looked again. There was nothing
there. Jan tried to stay calm as she pushed buttons on the radio. There was no
answer. The space station was gone.

Lesson 4 Use Describing Words

Now, write some sentences about the place you visited. Answer each question. Include at least one describing word in each sentence. Remember: A sentence must begin with a capital letter and end with an end mark.

What did you see? Was it very colorful, pretty, or ugly?

_____

_____

What did you hear? Were there many kinds of sounds, or just a few?

_____

_____

What did you touch? Was it hard, bumpy, or sticky?

_____

_____

What did you smell? Were there many smells, or just one?

_____

_____

Did you have something to eat? How did it taste?

_____

_____

Lesson 5 Write About Today

Every day something happens. On some
days, you do the same old things. On other
days, you do different things. It's fun to write
about what we do.

What have you done today? List what you have done.

_____   _____

_____   _____

_____   _____

Now, write some sentences about what you have done today.
Remember to use describing words so your readers can see, hear,
smell, feel, or taste what you did.

_____

_____

_____

_____

_____

_____

_____

Lesson 5 Write About Today

Now, list some things you know you will do later today.

_____   _____

_____   _____

Write about what you will do later today. Begin each sentence with a capital letter. End each sentence with a period.

_____

_____

_____

_____

_____

_____

_____

Now, look back at your sentences. Correct any that contain mistakes.

Questions to Ask About Descriptive Writing

Do your sentences include details?
Did you tell how something looked, sounded, smelled, felt, or tasted?
Does each sentence begin with a capital letter and end with an end mark?
Does each sentence have a complete thought?

son 5 Write About Today

at is your favorite part of the day? Is it morning? Or maybe it is
er school? Draw a picture of something you do during your favorite
art of the day.

What would you like to say about your favorite part of the day? Write
about what is happening in your picture. When you are finished, ask
yourself the questions on the bottom of page 17.

_____

_____

_____

_____

_____

_____

_____

Chapter 1 Post-Test

Write a title for this picture.

_____

Now, write a sentence about something you see in the picture. You may make up details about how something might look, sound, smell, feel, or taste.

_____

_____

Now, write a sentence about something you ate today. Include at least two details that tell how the food looked, sounded, smelled, felt, or tasted.

_____

_____

NAME _____

How do you feel today? Do you feel happy, sad, or excited? Draw a picture that shows how you feel.

Now, write a sentence about how you feel. Add details about why you feel this way.

_____

_____

Lesson 1 I Feel...

Imagine it is your birthday. You have a big outdoor party planned. Now, however, it is raining. How do you feel? Draw a picture. Then, write a sentence telling how you feel.

_____

_____

_____

_____

Pretend that you just won a 200-mile bike race. You are very tired, but very excited. Someone just handed you a huge trophy. How would you feel? Draw a picture. Then, write a sentence about it.

_____

_____

_____

_____

Lesson 2 I See a Place...

You see many places every day. What is one place you have seen today? Draw a picture of it. Then, write a sentence about the place. Use details to help your readers "see" the place.

_____

_____

Look back at your sentence. Does it begin with a capital letter? Does it end with a period? Is it a complete thought?

Lesson 2 | I See a Place...

Dean wrote a sentence about his bedroom.

The walls are blue and have many things on them.

Dean did not help you see his room very well, did he? The blue part is good, but what do "many things" look like? We cannot tell because we do not know what "things" are.

Dean writes a new sentence.

The walls are blue and have many posters on them.

Now can you see Dean's room? We do not know what is on the posters, but at least we know what is hanging on the walls.

Think about your room. Write a sentence to describe it. Use words that describe just what you want your readers to see.

_____

_____

Questions to Ask About Descriptive Writing

Do your sentences include details?
Did you tell how something looked, sounded, smelled, felt, or tasted?
Does each sentence begin with a capital letter and end with an end mark?
Does each sentence have a complete thought?

Lesson 2 I See a Place...

Make up a place. It might be the perfect bedroom. It might be a forest on a distant planet. Draw a picture of your made-up place. Then, write one or two sentences about your place.

_____

_____

_____

Lesson 3 When Did It Happen?

Finish the story. Draw the missing picture.

First

Next

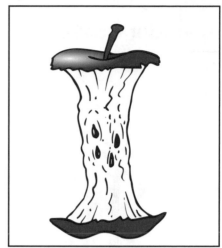

Last

First

Next

Last

Lesson 3 | When Did It Happen?

Look at the pictures. You can tell what happens first, next, and last. Label the pictures in order. Write **first**, **next**, and **last**. These are called **time-order words**.

_____   _____   _____

_____   _____   _____

Lesson 3 When Did It Happen?

Look at the pictures. You can tell what happens first, next, and last.
Label the pictures in order. Write **first**, **next**, and **last**. These are called
time-order words.

_____   _____   _____

_____   _____   _____

Lesson 4 Put It in Order

Now, write sentences to show the order of things.

Write one sentence about each picture. The first sentences are started for you.

First

Next

Last

First, _____

Next, _____

Last, _____

First

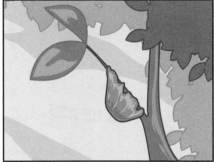
Next

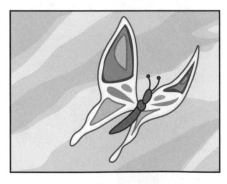
Last

_____

_____

_____

Lesson 4 Put It in Order

These pictures are not in the right order. First, label them **first**, **next**, and **last**. Next, write one sentence about each picture. Last, read your story out loud to see how it sounds.

_____   _____   _____

_____

_____

_____   _____   _____

_____

_____

Lesson 5 What Do You Know?

Martha made a list of the things she knows about the sky.

sky is blue	stars at night
sun during day	clouds day or night
moon at night	

There are some things Martha wants to find out about, though. She listed them here.

wind	puffy clouds
gray clouds	stringy clouds
white clouds	

What do you know about? Maybe you know about a certain animal or a maybe you know how to play many different kinds of games. Make a list of things you know about.

_____   _____

_____   _____

_____   _____

_____   _____

_____   _____

_____   _____

Lesson 5   What Do You Know?

Look back at the list you wrote on page 30. Choose one. Now, list what you know about it.

What I Know About: _____

_____   _____

_____   _____

_____   _____

_____   _____

What else would you like to find out about? List some things here.

_____   _____

_____   _____

_____   _____

_____   _____

Lesson 6 Find Out About It

One way to find out about something is to ask a question. Take a close look at this question.

What kind of cloud is that?

Circle the first letter of the question. It is a capital letter.

Circle the mark at the end of the question. It is a question mark.

Notice that the question is a complete thought.

Here is another question. Circle the capital letter at the beginning. Circle the question mark at the end.

Do you think it will rain?

Now, read this question. Something is missing. Add the question mark at the end.

When will the rain end

Greg corrected the next question. He knew that the first letter should be a capital letter. So, he drew three little lines under the letter and wrote the capital letter above it. He also added a question mark at the end.

D
do you see a rainbow?

Lesson 6 Find Out About It

What would you like to find out about the weather? Write your own question here.

_____

_____

Now, look at these pictures. Ask some questions. Some questions are started for you.

What color is _____

How big is _____

_____

_____

Questions to Ask About a Question

Does it begin with a capital letter?
Does it end with a question mark?
Does it tell a complete thought?

Now, look back at your questions. Correct any sentences that contain mistakes.

Lesson 6 Find Out About It

Emily wants to find out about many things.
She wrote some of her questions down.

what do pandas eat

Where is the sun at night

Correct Emily's questions. Look back at page 32 to see how to correct capital letters and question marks.

Now, write some of your own questions. What do you want to find out about? When you are finished, check your questions for capital letters and question marks. Make sure each question is a complete thought.

_____

_____

_____

_____

_____

_____

_____

_____

Chapter 2 Post-Test

Look at this picture.

Write a sentence about the place in the picture.

_____

_____

Ask a question about something you see in the picture.

_____

Look at the pictures. Write **first**, **next**, and **last** to show what order the pictures should be in. Then, write about the pictures. Use time-order words to help your readers understand.

_____ _____ _____

_____

_____

Chapter 3
Lesson 1 | This Is How

Sandy likes to make paper flowers. She wrote down the steps she uses to make them.

> Sandy used clear words so readers know exactly what to do.

> Sandy numbered the steps so the order is clear.

> Sandy included all of the steps.

Paper Flowers

1. First, cut tissue paper in squares.
2. Put the end of a pencil in the center of a paper square.
3. Wrap the paper around the pencil.
4. Remove the pencil.
5. Finally, put a green pipe cleaner on the bottom of the flower for a stem.

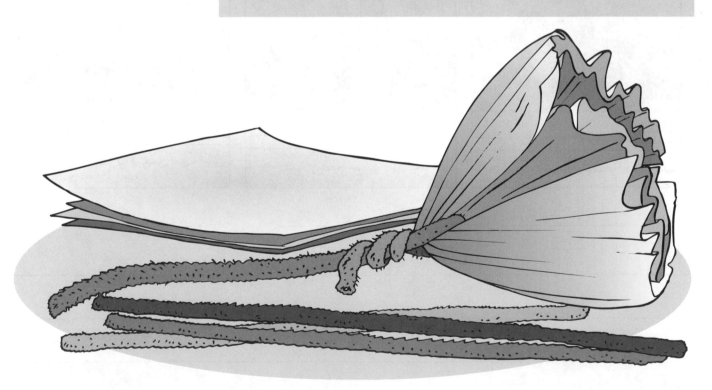

Lesson I This Is How

What do you know how to make or do? Maybe you know how to make something out of clay. Maybe you know how to plant flowers. Think of the steps it takes. Draw the steps in order. If you need more space, use another sheet of paper.

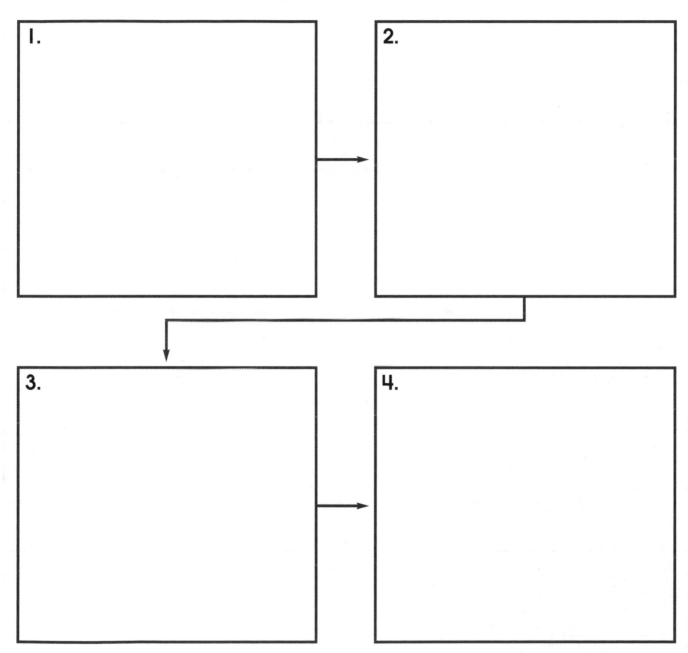

Lesson 1 This Is How

Look back at the pictures you drew on page 37. Now, write the steps. Remember to number your steps. Use clear words so that your readers know exactly what to do.

Lesson 2 You Are an Expert

Sandy already listed the steps for making paper flowers. Now, she wants to write a complete set of instructions. Here is what she wrote.

Sandy added describing words to be more clear.

Sandy L.

March 14

How to Make a Tissue Paper Flower

First, cut a square piece of ^colored tissue paper. For a small flower, use a 2-by-2-inch square. For a large flower, use a 5-by-5-inch square. Then, place the ^eraser end of a pencil in the center of a square. Next, wrap the paper ^gently around the pencil. Remove the pencil. Finally, ~~put~~ ^twist a green pipe cleaner onto the bottom of the flower for a stem.

Sandy changed **put** to **twist** because it tells what to do with the pipe cleaner.

Sandy added a word that tells how something should be done.

Lesson 2 You Are an Expert

Think again about what you know how to do. Use your idea from pages 37 and 38, or choose a different idea. Make sure you know all the steps. Write your steps here.

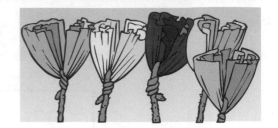

_____

_____

_____

_____

_____

_____

_____

_____

Questions to Ask About How-to Writing

Did you put the steps in order?

Did you include all of the steps?

Did you use order words to make the order clear?

Did you use clear words that tell what things look like or how to do things?

Does each sentence begin with a capital letter?

Does each sentence end with an end mark?

Lesson 2 You Are an Expert

Now, look back at your writing. Is there anything you want to change? Are the steps in order? Could you add words to make something more clear? Does every sentence help readers understand?

Write your directions again. Make them even better. When you finish writing, ask yourself the questions on the bottom of page 40.

_____

_____

_____

_____

_____

_____

_____

_____

_____

_____

Lesson 3 You Can't Miss It

How do you get to a new place? You might
follow a map or ask for directions. What if
someone asks you for directions? Would you
know how to give clear directions? Start by
writing some words that you might use to give
directions. Here are some words to help you
get started. If you get stuck, think about how
you get from one place to another.

first _____   right _____

next _____   left _____

then _____   above _____

last _____   below _____

finally _____   next to _____

_____   _____

_____   _____

_____   _____

_____   _____

_____   _____

_____   _____

Lesson 3 You Can't Miss It

Jim's mom is going to help the librarian at school tomorrow. She has asked Jim for directions to the library. Here is what Jim wrote.

> First, sign in at the table by the front door. Then, go straight ahead to the office. Turn right and go to the end of the hallway. Turn left and go to the third door on the left. Enter the library.

Jim gave his mom good directions. He used order words and many direction words.

Can you give directions to the library in your school? Close your eyes and imagine going from your school's front door to the library. Write the directions here.

_____

_____

_____

_____

_____

_____

_____

Lesson 3 You Can't Miss It

Now, give directions to another place in your school. Help someone find your classroom, the lunchroom, the gym, or another area of the school that you like. Remember to use time-order words as well as direction words. Look back at your list on page 42 if you want to.

_____

_____

_____

_____

_____

_____

_____

_____

_____

Look back at what you wrote. Make sure that each sentence begins with a capital letter and ends with a period.

Lesson 4 It Happened Because...

Why was Tess late for school? Why didn't Johnny turn in his homework? Why does the wind blow? When we write, we often tell why things happen.

Look at some pictures. The first picture shows what happened. The second picture shows why it happened.

This happened...   because...

Now, write **This happened** or **because** under the correct picture.

_____   _____

Lesson 4 It Happened Because...

Now, write about why things happen. Look at the pictures. Then, complete the sentence.

This happened...   because...

_____ because

_____.

Did something happen to you today? Why did it happen? Draw what happened. Then, draw a picture that shows why it happened. Finally, write a sentence about what happened and why.

This happened...   because...

_____

_____

Lesson 5 Explain It

When we write, we often tell, or explain, what happened. We usually tell what happened, and we tell why it happened. First, practice telling why. Answer these questions. Remember to put a period at the end of each sentence.

Why were you late?

I was late because _____

_____

_____

_____

Why are your shoes dirty?

_____

_____

_____

Why do you like that book?

_____

_____

_____

Lesson 5 Explain It

Imagine that your picture is in the newspaper. Why would you like your picture to be in the newspaper? Did you invent something? Are you a hero? First, complete the sentence to tell why your picture is in the paper.

My picture is in the paper because _____

_____.

Now, explain everything that happened. Give lots of details.

_____

_____

_____

_____

_____

_____

_____

_____

_____

Lesson 5 Explain It

Look back at what you wrote on page 48. Use this checklist to check your writing.

_____ Does each sentence begin with a capital letter?

_____ Does each sentence end with an end mark?

_____ Did you tell clearly what happened?

_____ Did you explain why it happened?

_____ Did you tell events in the order in which they happened?

_____ Did you use words to help your readers "see" what happened?

Think about how you can make your writing better. Write about your newspaper picture again. Make changes so your writing will be even better. Write a new copy here.

_____

_____

_____

_____

_____

_____

Lesson 6 The Writing Process: Friendly Letter

When you write a letter to a friend or grandparent, you are writing a friendly letter. It is fun to write friendly letters. It's even more fun to get them. Maybe if you send a friendly letter, you will get one back.

Tina wrote a friendly letter to her cousin Alice. As you read, think about why Tina wrote this letter.

July 17

Dear Alice,
    I just read your letter, and I am so excited. Mom and Dad are excited, too. You haven't been here for more than a year.
    I can't wait until you see my room. I got a bunk bed because Emily got her own room. You can have the top bunk!
    There are only 16 more days until you get here.
            Love,
            Tina

Tina wrote this letter because _____.

_____.

I might write a friendly letter because _____

_____.

Lesson 6 The Writing Process: Friendly Letter

Look at Tina's letter again.

There is always a comma after the person's name.

There is a **date** at the top.

This is the **greeting**. The word **Dear** always begins with a capital letter.

July 17

Dear Alice,

I just read your letter, and I am so excited. Mom and Dad are excited, too. You haven't been here for more than a year.

I can't wait until you see my room. I got a bunk bed because Emily got her own room. You can have the top bunk!

There are only 16 more days until you get here.

Love,
Tina

This is the **body** of the letter.

This is the **closing**. The word may be different, but there is always a comma after the word.

The person writing the letter always signs his or her name.

Questions to Ask About a Friendly Letter

Is there a date?
Does the greeting begin with Dear?
Is there a comma after the person's name in the greeting?
Is there a comma after the closing?
Did you sign your name?

Lesson 6 The Writing Process: Friendly Letter

Think of someone you know. Write a letter to that person. Start with the greeting. Next, write the body of the letter. Then, write the closing. Look back at Tina's letter on pages 50 and 51 if you need to. In your letter, tell about something that happened and explain why. This will be your first draft. Later, you will have a chance to make your letter better and write a final copy.

_____

_____

_____

_____

_____

_____

_____

_____

_____

_____

Lesson 6 The Writing Process: Friendly Letter

Now, look back at your letter on page 52. Is there anything you want to change? Could you add words that tell how something feels or looks?

Write your letter again. Make it even better. When you finish writing, ask yourself the questions on the bottom of page 51. This will be your final draft.

_____

_____

_____

_____

_____

_____

_____

_____

_____

_____

_____

Chapter 3 Post-Test

Tell how to fix a bowl of cereal for breakfast. Think about what you do. Then, write the steps here.

First, _____

_____.

Next, _____

_____.

Last, _____

_____.

It is your turn to do the dishes. A friend offers to help you do the job. Give directions so your friend knows where to put the dishes. Tell your friend how to get from the sink to the correct place in the kitchen. Use order words and direction words to make your directions clear.

a drinking glass _____

_____

_____

a fork _____

_____

_____

Chapter 3 Post-Test

Write a friendly letter to someone you know. Tell about something funny or odd that has happened to you. Remember to include these parts: a date, a greeting, a body, and a closing.

_____

_____

_____

_____

_____

_____

_____

_____

_____

_____

_____

_____

_____

_____

_____

Chapter 4

Lesson 1 Your Five Senses

We use our senses to learn about the things around us. Sometimes we use one sense. At other times, we use many senses. These are your five senses: **seeing**, **hearing**, **smelling**, **touching**, and **tasting**. How do you use them? Look at each picture. Circle the senses you could use to learn about the object in the picture.

seeing   hearing   smelling

touching   tasting

seeing   hearing   smelling

touching   tasting

seeing   hearing   smelling

touching   tasting

Lesson 1 Your Five Senses

Imagine that you are one of the people in this picture. Use your senses to learn about everything around you. Write what you see, hear, smell, touch, and taste.

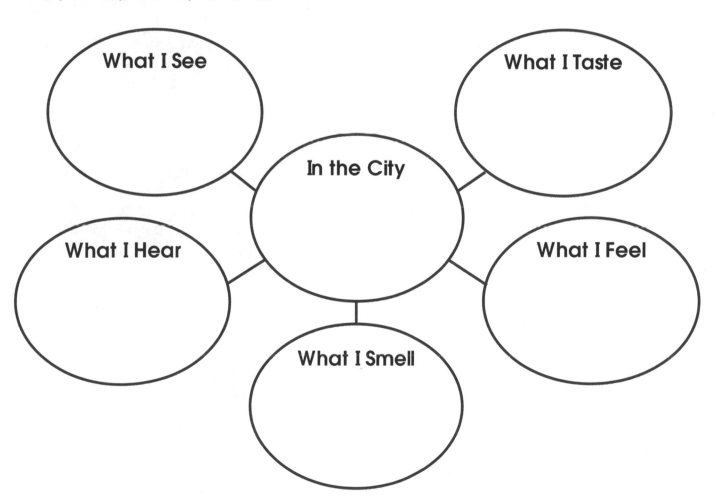

Lesson 1 Your Five Senses

Look at each picture. Name one sense you could use to learn about the object in the picture. Then, write a describing word that tells what you would learn from that sense. The first one is done for you.

___touch___   ___rough___

_____   _____

_____   _____

_____   _____

Lesson 2 Describe It

Kay's family is camping. Kay is going to use all of her senses to describe their tent.

I see <u>big, blue</u>

I hear <u>zipping zipper</u>

I smell <u>plastic, campfire smoke</u>

I feel <u>smooth</u>

I taste <u>yuck—don't try it</u>

Kay visits a nature center. There are many things to see and touch. Circle one of the items shown here. Imagine that you can see, hear, smell, and touch it. Write good describing words.

I see _____

_____

I hear _____

_____

I smell _____

_____

I feel _____

_____

Lesson 2 Describe It

Pretend that this pizza is sitting on the table in front of you. You have just taken your first bite. Write words that tell what you see, hear, smell, feel, and taste.

I see _____

_____

_____

I hear _____

_____

I smell _____

_____

I feel _____

_____

I taste _____

_____

Lesson 2 Describe It

You can use many of these good describing words in a sentence. Here is a sentence that Kay wrote about the frog that she touched at the nature center.

The frog's slimy skin was cool, and his body was soft.

Think about that pizza again. Look at the words you wrote on page 60. Write a sentence about the pizza. Try to use at least two of the describing words in your sentence.

_____

_____

Now, think about another food that you like to eat. How does it look, sound, smell, feel, and taste? Write the name of the food. Then, write a sentence about that food. Use at least two describing words so your reader can really "see" the food.

Food _____

_____

_____

Look at the room around you. Choose an object. If you can, touch it. Look at it from all sides. Write the name of the object. Then, write a sentence about it. Use words that show that you used at least two senses to learn about the object.

Object _____

_____

Lesson 3 Create a Riddle

Here is a riddle: What is bigger than a car, gray, wrinkly, and has big ears?

Did you guess an elephant?

Here is another one: What is smaller than a cat, gray, soft, and has big ears?

Did you guess a mouse? The describing words gave it away, didn't they?

Here are some more riddles for you to solve. Some of them are tricky. The pictures might help.

What is long, round, skinny, very light, and easy to bend?

_____

What is long and skinny, has a light on the front, and moves very fast?

_____

What is long, round, sometimes skinny and sometimes fat, and pointed on one end?

_____

What is long, round, heavy, hard, and used to be alive?

_____

Lesson 3 Create a Riddle

You can make riddles, too. Just use your senses!

Start with riddles about objects in the room around you. Look around and find something interesting. Tell what it looks like, sounds like, smells like, feels like, or tastes like. All of these describing words help you write a riddle. Remember to put a question mark at the end of each riddle.

What is _____

_____

_____

Answer _____

What is _____

_____

_____

Answer _____

Now, write one more riddle about something in the room. Do not write the answer this time. Give your riddle to a friend or family member. Can that person guess the answer to your riddle?

What is _____

_____

_____

Lesson 3 Create a Riddle

Riddles can be funny or tricky. Try this one.

What is bigger than a car, has blue and white stripes, and has big ears?

It is an elephant in striped pajamas.

Here is another one:

What is red on top, blue on the bottom, and purple in the middle?

It is me, after I spilled grape juice on myself,

Use your imagination to think up your own funny or tricky riddles. Remember to use good describing words. Ask a friend to solve the riddles.

What is _____

_____

Answer _____

What is _____

_____

Answer _____

What is _____

_____

Answer _____

Lesson 4 I Can Imagine

What if you could create a new planet? Would your planet have mountains? Would there be fields of corn? Would it have forests or oceans? Where would people live? Close your eyes and imagine a place on your new planet. Write some words that tell what you "see" in this place.

_____   _____

_____   _____

_____   _____

_____   _____

Imagine your planet again. What colors do you see? What do you hear and smell? What do things feel like? Write some words that tell how your planet looks, sounds, smells, and feels.

_____   _____

_____   _____

_____   _____

Lesson 4 I Can Imagine

Look back at the words you wrote on page 65. Tell about your planet. Write one or two sentences to answer each question. Remember to use your senses as you describe your planet.

What is the most beautiful part of your planet?

_____

_____

_____

What does a house look like on your planet?

_____

_____

_____

Are there plants? If I touched one, what would it feel like?

_____

_____

_____

What does the sky look like on your planet?

_____

_____

_____

Lesson 4 I Can Imagine

You want a friend to move to your planet with you. Tell the friend all about the place in a letter. If you need to, look at page 51 to see the four parts of a friendly letter.

_____

_____

_____

_____

_____

_____

_____

_____

_____

_____

Questions to Ask About a Friendly Letter

Is there a date?
Does the greeting begin with **Dear**?
Is there a comma after the person's name in the greeting?
Is there a comma after the closing?
Did you sign your name?

Lesson 5 Compare Them

When we think about how two things are the same and different, we compare them. Look at these pictures. Then, complete the sentences.

 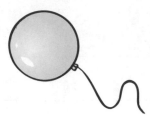

These balloons are the same _____.

These balloons are different _____.

These cars are the same _____.

These cars are different _____.

These horses are the same _____.

These horses are different _____.

Lesson 5 Compare Them

Compare these boats. How are they the same? How are they
different?

The first boat _____.

The second boat _____.

What is the same about these boys? What is
different? Complete the sentences.

The first boy _____.

The second boy _____.

Now, compare your own hair color with the hair color of a friend or
classmate. Complete these sentences.

My hair is _____.

The other person's hair is _____.

Are your hair colors the same or different?

Our hair colors are _____.

Lesson 5 Compare Them

These fish are the same size. What else about them can you compare? List some things here.

_____   _____

_____   _____

_____   _____

Tell what is the same about the fish.

Both fish have _____.

Tell what is different about the fish.

One fish has _____,

but the other fish has _____.

On Your Own

It is fun to compare things. Compare a playground ball with an orange. Compare a banana with a telephone. Choose two things and compare them. Make a list of how they are the same and how they are different on a separate piece of paper.

Lesson 6 Use Comparing Words

Compare these spiders. Tell which spider is bigger and which is smaller.

The first spider is _____.

The second spider is _____.

Look at these pictures. Read the sentences.

The first ladder is **taller than** the second ladder.

The second ladder is **shorter than** the first ladder.

Now, use the words **taller than** and **shorter than** to compare these pictures. Complete the sentences.

Dad is _____ Timmy.

Timmy is _____ Dad.

Lesson 6 Use Comparing Words

Look at these pictures. Use the words **faster than** and **slower than** to complete the sentences.

A bird is _____ a plane.

A plane is _____ a bird.

A car is _____ a bike.

A bike is _____ a car.

Now, draw your own pictures. Show something that is faster than or slower than something else. Then, use the words **faster than** and **slower than** in two sentences about your pictures.

_____

_____

Lesson 6 Use Comparing Words

Look at the pictures. Write sentences that compare the objects in the pictures.

_____

_____

_____

_____

_____

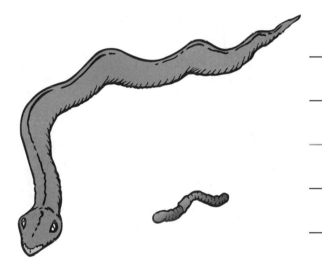

_____

_____

_____

_____

_____

_____

_____

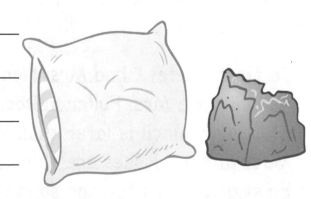

Lesson 7 Alike and Different

Cayla is in second grade. In some ways, second grade is the same as first grade. In other ways, it is different. Cayla drew a chart and wrote down her ideas.

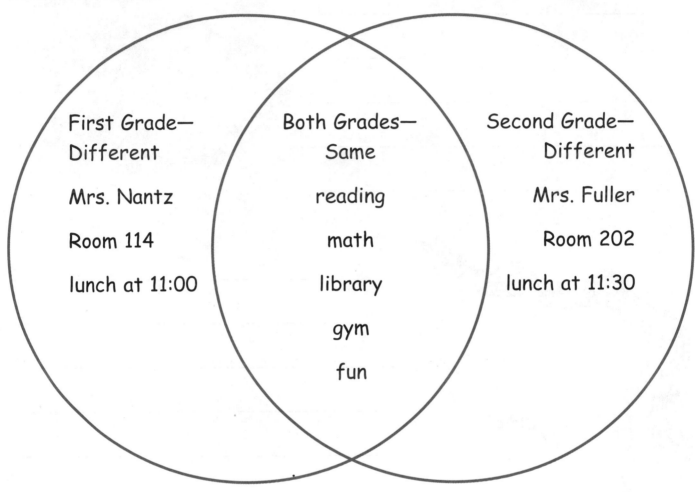

First Grade—
Different

Mrs. Nantz

Room 114

lunch at 11:00

Both Grades—
Same

reading

math

library

gym

fun

Second Grade—
Different

Mrs. Fuller

Room 202

lunch at 11:30

After she made her chart, Cayla wrote some sentences about first and second grade.

In first grade, I had Mrs. Nantz in Room 114.
Now, I have Mrs. Fuller in Room 202.
This year, lunch is later than last year.
Most of the classes are the same.
First grade was fun and so is second grade.

Lesson 7 Alike and Different

Think back to last year. What did you do in first grade? What did you learn? Write down everything you can remember.

_____   _____

_____   _____

_____   _____

Now, think about what is happening in second grade. How is second grade different from first grade? How are the grades the same? Write your ideas in the chart. If you need to, look back at Cayla's chart on page 74.

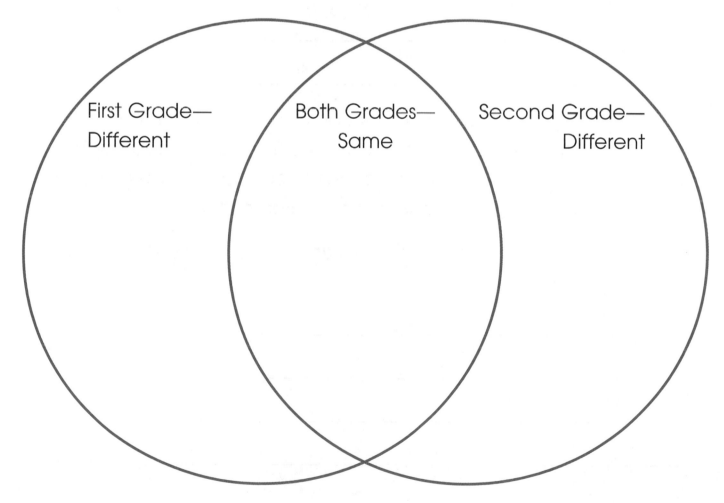

Lesson 7 Alike and Different

Now, write some sentences that compare first grade and second grade. Use the ideas you wrote in the chart on page 75.

_____

_____

_____

_____

_____

_____

Look at your sentences again. Does each one begin with a capital letter? Does each one end with a period? Did you use good words to describe how something looked, sounded, or felt? Did you use any comparing words, such as **better than** or **later than**?

Think of how you could make some of your sentences better. Write one or two of them here.

_____

_____

_____

_____

Lesson 8 The Writing Process: Thank-You Note

People write friendly letters for many reasons. One reason might be to thank someone for a gift. Here is a thank-you note that Brett wrote to his aunt.

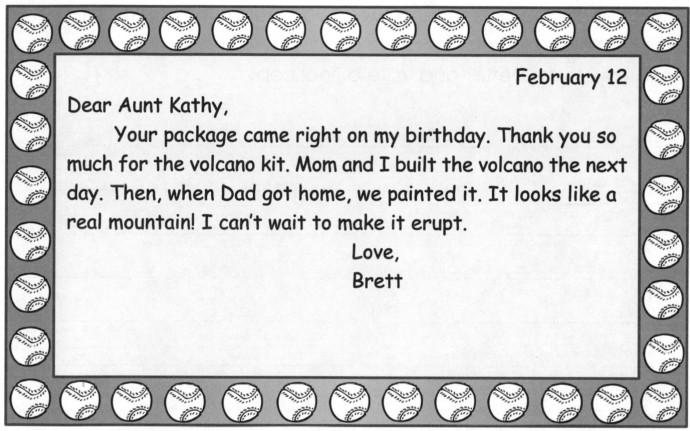

February 12

Dear Aunt Kathy,
    Your package came right on my birthday. Thank you so much for the volcano kit. Mom and I built the volcano the next day. Then, when Dad got home, we painted it. It looks like a real mountain! I can't wait to make it erupt.
                Love,
                Brett

Brett thanked his aunt nicely. He used the four parts of a friendly letter: date, greeting, body, and closing. He also told his aunt how he used her gift. Then, Brett wrote something special about the gift. He helped her "see" the gift by saying that "it looks like a real mountain!"

Think of some gifts you have received, or would like to receive. List them here.

_____   _____

_____   _____

Lesson 8 The Writing Process: Thank-You Note

Now, write a thank-you note for one of the gifts you listed on page 77. Start with the date and the greeting. Then, write the body. Remember to thank the person and to say something special about the gift. Use words to help the person "see" what you mean. Then, write the closing. This will be your first draft. Later, you will have a chance to make your letter better and write a final copy.

_____

_____

_____

_____

_____

_____

_____

Questions to Ask About a Thank-You Note

Is there a date?
Does the greeting begin with Dear?
Is there a comma after the person's name in the greeting?
Do you thank the person and name the gift?
Is there a comma after the closing?
Did you sign your name?

Lesson 8 The Writing Process: Thank-You Note

Now, look back at the draft of your thank-you note. Ask yourself the questions at the bottom of page 78. How can you make the note better? Could you add words that tell how something feels or looks?

Write your thank-you note again. Make it even better. When you finish writing, ask yourself the questions on the bottom of page 78 again.

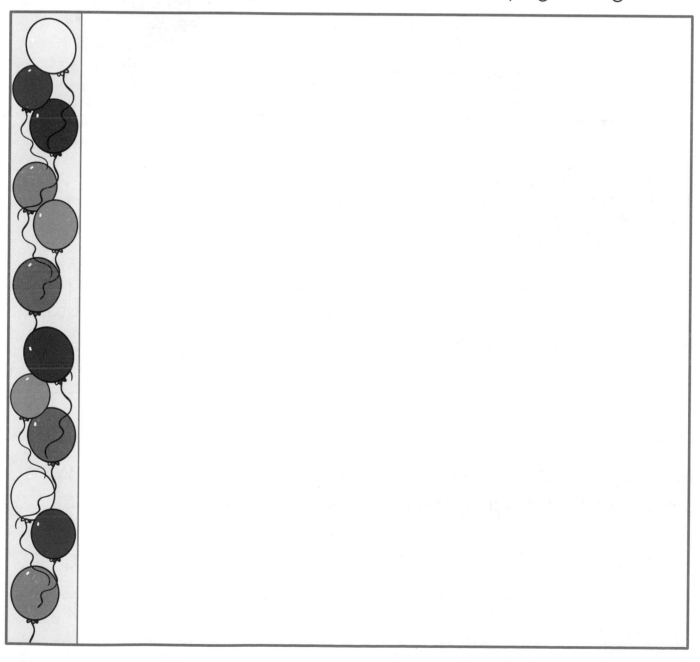

Chapter 4 Post-Test

Look at each picture. Tell what senses you could use to learn about each item.

_____

_____

_____

_____

_____

_____

_____

_____

Now, look back at the picture of the dog. Imagine that the dog is right beside you. Write a sentence about the dog. Use sense words that tell how the dog sounds or feels.

_____

_____

Look at the picture of the food. Imagine that you are eating it. Write sentences that describe the food. Use all five senses.

_____

_____

_____

Chapter 4 Post-Test

Look at the picture. Complete the sentence.

The first computer is _____
the second computer.

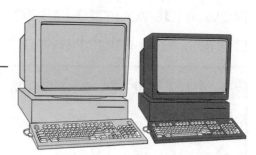

What is the same about these computers?
What is different about them? Fill in the chart.

First Computer—
Different

Both Computers—
Same

Second Computer—
Different

Use what you wrote in the chart to write some sentences about the
computers. Tell how they are the same. Tell how they are different.

_____

_____

_____

_____

Chapter 5

NAME _____

Now that you are in second grade, you have already read lots of stories. You might even have written some stories. What is a story?

> A story tells about people or animals. They are the **characters** in the story.
>
> A good story is **fun** for the reader to read.
>
> A story has a **beginning**, a **middle**, and an **end**.
>
> A good story has **describing words** that tell about the characters, where the story takes place, and what happens.

Read this story. Think about what happens at the beginning, in the middle, and at the end.

A Day with Dad

Today is Saturday. Sue's mom has a meeting. So, Sue and Dad will spend the day together. Sue wonders what they will do.

First, Dad washes the dishes. Sue watches because she cannot reach. Then, Dad cleans the blue rug. Sue watches because the machine is too big. After that, Dad washes dirty windows. Sue watches because the windows are too high.

By lunchtime, Dad is worn out from working. Sue is worn out from watching. What can Sue do? Then, she has a great idea. Sue invites Dad to her room for lunch. Dad can just fit on Sue's little chair. And Sue can reach everything. It is the best lunch ever.

Lesson 1 What Is a Story?

Answer these questions about "A Day with Dad." Look back at the story on page 82 if you need to.

Who are the characters in the story?

_____   _____

What happens at the beginning, in the middle, and at the end of the story?

Beginning

Middle

End

How does the writer describe the rug and windows? Find these and other describing words. List them here.

_____   _____

_____   _____

Lesson 2 Write About It

In a story, writers usually tell what happens in order. First, one thing happens. Then, another thing happens, and so on. Practice telling about things that happen in order.

What is happening in these pictures?

First, _____

Then, _____

Notice how the words **first** and **then** help keep things in order. Now, write two sentences about what is happening in these pictures. Use time-order words to tell the order in which things happen.

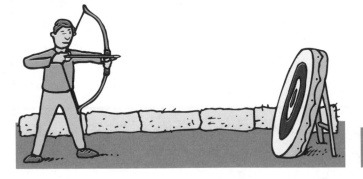 

_____

_____

Lesson 2 Write About It

Now that you have everything in order, think about making your sentences interesting. Use details that help your readers "see" what is happening. Let's look at these two pictures again. Imagine you are writing a story about what is happening.

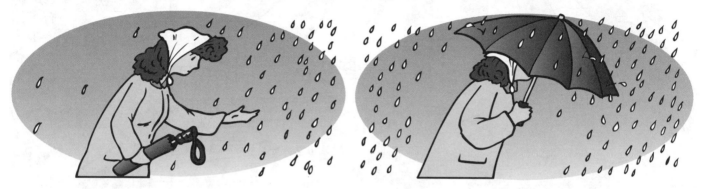

Write two more sentences about these pictures. Use words that tell how something looks, sounds, smells, feels, or tastes.

_____

_____

_____

Think about where this woman is. How might this place sound or feel or smell? Write a sentence about it.

_____

_____

Finally, write a sentence about the woman in the picture. How does she look or what sounds could she be hearing?

_____

Lesson 3 Write a Story

Look at the picture. Think of a story you might write about the people or the place in the picture.

These people are the characters in your story. Think of names for several of them.

_____   _____

_____   _____

Where are these people? Write some words that tell where they are. Also, write some describing words that tell about the sights, sounds, and smells of the place.

_____   _____

_____   _____

_____   _____

_____   _____

Lesson 3 Write a Story

Look at the picture on page 86 again. In the boxes, write ideas about what will happen in the beginning, in the middle, and at the end of your story.

Beginning

Middle

End

Lesson 3 Write a Story

Write your story here. Look back at the ideas you wrote on pages 86 and 87. Remember to give your story a title. When you finish, read your story and ask yourself the questions at the bottom of the page. If you can find ways to make your story better, write it again on another sheet of paper.

_____

_____

_____

_____

_____

_____

_____

_____

Questions to Ask About a Story

Does the story have a beginning, a middle, and an end?
Did you use time-order words to make the order of events clear?
Did you use words that tell how things look, sound, smell, feel, and taste?
Is the story fun for your readers?
Does each sentence have a complete thought?

Lesson 4 I Saw It All!

It is fun to tell about things that we have seen. Maybe you saw an interesting bird. Or, maybe you saw an amazing play at a football or baseball game.

Chase saw something amazing happen yesterday. Today at school, he wrote about it. First, he wrote down a few things to keep his ideas in order.

game with Mom
rain then wind
tree bending
back and forth
crack

Then, Chase wrote about what he saw. Here is his first draft.

    It started to rain, and Mom called me into the house. We sat by the big window and played a game. Pretty soon, it started to get windy. We planted some new trees in the back yard last week. We watched the tree in the front yard. It bent back and forth. The wind blew the branches around. All of a sudden there was a huge crack. Mom and I saw the tree fall. Now, our big tree is lying across the yard. Mom says the tree was old and rotten inside.

Look back at Chase's notes. Did he use those ideas in his writing? Find and circle them in Chase's first draft.

Lesson 4 I Saw It All!

Chase read his draft again. He decided he could make it better. He added words to help his readers see how the tree looked, both before it fell and as it fell. He also found a sentence that didn't belong. And he added a new beginning and a new ending.

I was playing outside yesterday after school.
  ^It started to rain, and Mom called me into the house. We sat by

the big window and played a game. Pretty soon, it started to get

windy. ~~We planted some new trees in the back yard last week.~~ We
        big oak
watched the ^tree in the front yard. It bent back and forth. The
  whipped
wind ~~blew~~ the branches around. All of a sudden there was a huge
          slowly twist and
crack. Mom and I saw the tree ^fall. Now, our big tree is lying across
                                                I will miss that
the yard. Mom says the tree was old and rotten inside. ^   tree.

Think about something you have seen. Maybe it was something funny or something unusual or something surprising. Write a few ideas here about what you saw. You might include some words that tell how something looked, sounded, smelled, felt, or tasted.

_____   _____

_____   _____

_____   _____

Lesson 4 I Saw It All!

Now, write about what you saw. Look back at what you wrote on page 90 to keep your ideas in order. Remember to include describing words so readers know how things looked, sounded, or smelled.

_____

_____

_____

_____

_____

_____

_____

_____

_____

Read your writing. Can you make it better? Can you make it more interesting? Are there any ideas or sentences that don't belong? Make changes to your writing, like Chase did on page 90. Then, read your writing out loud to see how it sounds.

Lesson 5 The Writing Process: Story

"The Three Little Pigs" and "Snow White" are fairy tales. You probably know those and many other fairy tales as well. Sometimes it is fun to start with a story that everyone knows, and then make a new story about what happened next. For example, what happened to the Three Little Pigs? Did they all stay in the brick house? Where did the wolf go? And what about Snow White? What happened while she and the prince were living happily ever after? Did they ever visit the dwarfs? Or did the dwarfs go and live with Snow White?

Which fairy tales do you like best? Write their names here.

_____   _____

_____   _____

Think about how the fairy tales end. Ask yourself what happens next. Do you get any good ideas? Choose one fairy tale that you want to continue. Write its name and the names of the characters here.

Fairy tale _____

Characters _____

How does the fairy tale end? _____

_____

Write some ideas here about how you will add to the fairy tale.

_____

_____

Lesson 5 The Writing Process: Story

You are writing a story, so you need to have a beginning, a middle, and an end. Keep these things in mind:

- In the beginning of a story, readers meet the characters and find out there is a problem.

- In the middle, the action of the story takes place. The characters decide how to solve the problem.

- At the end, the problem is solved.

What will happen in the beginning, middle, and end of your new fairy tale?

Beginning

Middle

End

Write the first draft of your fairy tale on page 94. When you are finished, ask yourself the questions at the bottom of the page. Then, make your story better. You may make changes on page 94, or write a new copy on a clean sheet of paper.

Lesson 5 The Writing Process: Story

_____

_____

_____

_____

_____

_____

_____

_____

_____

Questions to Ask About a Story

Does the story have a beginning, a middle, and an end?

Did you use time-order words to make the order of events clear?

Did you use describing words that tell how things look, sound, smell, feel, and taste?

Is the story fun for your readers?

Does each sentence begin with a capital letter and end with an end mark?

Does each sentence have a complete thought?

Chapter 5 Post-Test

What is a story? Complete these sentences.

     A story tells about people or animals. They are the
_____ in the story. A good story is _____
for the reader to read. A story has three parts: a _____,
a _____, and an _____. A good story
has _____ words that tell about the characters, where
the story takes place, and what happens.

Write two sentences about these pictures. Use time-order words to
keep things in order.

 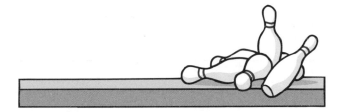

_____

_____

_____

Now, look at the two pictures again. This time, imagine you are there.
What do you see, hear, smell, feel, or taste? Write two sentences. Use
sense words to make the sentences interesting for your readers.

_____

_____

_____

Chapter 5 Post-Test

Look at the pictures on page 84 again. Choose one set of pictures and write a story using those characters and that place. Before you begin, write some notes about what happens at the beginning, in the middle, and at the end. If you need more room for your story, keep writing on another sheet of paper.

Beginning _____

Middle _____

End _____

_____

_____

_____

_____

_____

_____

_____

_____

_____

_____

Writer's Handbook

When should I use a capital letter?

The first word of a sentence always begins with a capital letter.

> **T**he kitten jumped into my lap.

The word **I** is always spelled with a capital letter.

> Kristen and **I** laughed at the kitten.

The name of a person or an animal always begins with a capital letter.

> The kitten belongs to **K**ristin.
> The kitten's name is **M**eep.

Other kinds of names also begin with capital letters. Here are some examples:

> streets: **M**artin **A**venue   **J**effers **R**oad
> schools: **J**ackson **E**lementary **S**chool
> towns and cities: **M**edford   **R**ome
> states: **W**isconsin   **G**eorgia
> countries: **C**anada   **I**taly
> holidays: **L**abor **D**ay
> days and months: **T**uesday   **J**uly
> clubs and groups: **C**ub **S**couts   **V**alley **G**arden **C**lub
> companies: **D**oggie **D**ay **C**are   **F**oster **P**aint **C**ompany

What are the rules about sentences?

A sentence must always tell a complete thought.

> Complete thought: She meowed.
> Complete thought: The kitten yawned and rolled over.
> Not a complete thought: She again.
> Not a complete thought: Around and around her.

Writer's Handbook

A sentence always begins with a capital letter.

      Carry the kitten carefully.

A sentence always ends with an end mark. There are three kinds of end marks. A sentence that tells something ends with a period.

      The kitten is soft**.**

A sentence that asks something ends with a question mark.

      Is the kitten soft**?**

A sentence that shows excitement or fear ends with an exclamation point.

      The kitten scratched me**!**

What is the writing process?

Writers use five steps when they write. These steps make up the writing **process**.

Step 1: Prewrite

First, writers think up ideas. This is called **pre-writing**. They might write their ideas in a list. They might even make a chart and put their ideas in order.

Sam will write about his trip to the zoo. He put his ideas in a web.

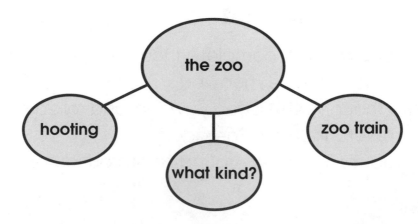

Writer's Handbook

Step 2: Draft

Next, writers put their ideas on paper. This is called a **first draft**. Writers know that there might be mistakes. That's okay. Most writers do not get everything perfect on the first try.

Here is Sam's first draft.

Zoo Noises

Every time I go, I learn something new. I went to the zoo three times last year. last week, I learned that there are many noises at the zoo. There was a funny hooting sound. I asked what kind that was Then, my brother told me it was the train whistle. I felt pretty silly. I wonder what I will learn next time I go to the zoo.

Step 3: Revise

Then, writers change or fix their first draft. This is called **revising**. They might move ideas around or add information. They might take out words or sentences that don't belong. Here are the changes that Sam made.

Zoo Noises

to the zoo
Every time I go, I learn something new. ~~I went to the zoo three~~ ~~times last year.~~ last week, I learned that there are many noises at the of animal
zoo. There was a funny hooting sound. I asked what kind that was Then, my brother told me it was the train whistle. I felt pretty silly.

I wonder what I will learn next time I go to the zoo.

Writer's Handbook

Step 4: Proofread

Writers usually write a new copy so their writing is neat. Then, they look again to make sure everything is correct. They look for mistakes in their sentences. This is called **proofreading**.

Sam wrote a new copy. Then, he found two last mistakes.

Zoo Noises

    Every time I go to the zoo, I learn something new. last week, I learned that there are many strange noises at the zoo. I heard a funny hooting sound. I asked what kind of animal that was⊙Then, my brother told me it was the train whistle. I felt pretty silly. I wonder what I will learn next time I go to the zoo.

Step 5: Publish

Finally, writers make a final copy that has no mistakes. They are now ready to share their writing with a reader. They might choose to read their writing out loud. They can add pictures and create a book. There are many ways for writers to **publish**, or share, their work with readers.

Here is the final copy of Sam's writing about the zoo.

Zoo Noises

    Every time I go to the zoo, I learn something new. Last week, I learned that there are many strange noises at the zoo. I heard a funny hooting sound. I asked what kind of animal that was. Then, my brother told me it was the train whistle. I felt pretty silly. I wonder what I will learn next time I go to the zoo.

Writer's Handbook

What different kinds of writing are there?

Writers sometimes write about things they have done or seen. They might tell about something funny, sad, or unusual. When Sam wrote about what he saw at the zoo, he was writing about real things that he did and saw.

Look at Sam's zoo story again.

The word **I** shows that the writer was part of the action.

Describing words help readers "see" or "hear" what is happening.

A time order word shows the order of events.

The writer stayed on topic. All of the sentences give more information about a zoo noise.

Zoo Noises
Every time I go to the zoo, I learn something new. Last week, I learned that there are many strange noises at the zoo. I heard a funny hooting sound. I asked what kind of animal that was. Then, my brother told me it was the train whistle. I felt pretty silly. I wonder what I will learn next time I go to the zoo.

Writers sometimes write about made-up things. They might write about people or animals. The people and animals might seem real, but the writers made them up. Here is a made-up story that Shawn wrote.

Time order words help keep ideas in order.

Shawn's readers will have fun reading his ideas.

Describing words help readers "see" what is happening.

The writer stayed on topic. All of the sentences give more information about a made-up zoo.

Shawn's Zoo
Shawn wants to be a zookeeper. Right now, he keeps small animals. He pretends that his mice and his cat are zoo animals.
Some day, he will keep big animals. He watches his gray mice running on their little wheel. At his zoo, Shawn will teach elephants to run on a big wheel. His cat chases a ball. At Shawn's zoo, the lions will play soccer against the tigers.
Shawn has lots of ideas for his zoo. He thinks his zoo will be a great zoo.

Writer's Handbook

Writers sometimes write about how to do things. They might tell how to play a game or make a snack. Sam has a favorite snack. He wrote about how to make it.

The steps are all in order, starting with the items needed to make the snack.

Order words help readers keep the steps in order.

Clear words help readers understand what to do.

Cracker-Cheese Surprise

First, set out wheat crackers, sliced olives, sliced cheese, and a metal pie plate. Lay out some crackers in the pie plate. Then, place one olive slice on each cracker. Place one slice of cheese on top of each cracker. Finally, ask a grown-up to set the pie plate under a broiler. Heat just until the cheese bubbles. Have the grown-up remove plate from broiler and let cool for several minutes. At last, you get to enjoy your healthy snack.

Writers sometimes write to describe things. They might tell about an object, a place, or an event. They use good sense, or describing, words so that readers can see, hear, smell, feel, or taste whatever is being described. Read how Sam described his snack.

Sizzle helps readers hear what is happening.

Warm helps readers know how the snack feels.

Bubbly helps readers see what is happening.

Salty helps readers taste the snack.

I can tell when my snack is done because I hear a little sizzle from the oven. When my mom opens the broiler door, the cheese is bubbly. I can hardly wait for the crackers to cool. When I take a bite, the cracker crunches and the warm cheese stretches out in a long string like taffy. And then, that salty little olive slice is just waiting to surprise me. Yum!

Writer's Handbook

Writers write friendly letters to share news or ideas. They also write letters to get information. A friendly letter has four parts: the date, the greeting, the body, and the closing. Here is a letter Sam wrote to a friend about something that happened at the zoo.

Words in the greeting each begin with a capital letter.

There is always a comma after the person's name.

The date is in the upper, right corner.

The body of the letter gives information.

Only the first word of the closing begins with a capital letter. There is always a comma after the closing.

The writer signs his or her name.

August 26

Dear Kyle,

Last week, while you were at camp, we went to the zoo. We had a great time.

The best part was the elephants. Did you know that elephants love to take baths? The elephant keeper was spraying a hose at the elephants. The water shot up in a big spout. The elephants stood under the water just as if they were taking a shower. Then, one of them started to dance. Before long, all three of them were dancing in the shower!

It's only a week until school starts. I'll show you my dancing elephant pictures on the first day of school.

Your friend,
Sam

Answer Key

Chapter 1

Lesson 1

Page 5
Circled titles:
A Sunny Day
Too Much Traffic
Circus in Town

Page 6
Answers will vary.

Lesson 2

Page 7
Circled titles:
Holly's Day
Mix-Up Day

Page 8
Space Race
No One at Home

Page 9
Answers will vary.

Lesson 3

Page 10
Answers will vary.

Page 11
Sentences will vary.

Page 12
Sentences will vary.

Lesson 4

Page 13
We ate buttery popcorn and salty
 peanuts.

Page 14
Answers will vary.

Page 15
Sentences will vary.

Lesson 5

Page 16
Answers will vary.

Page 17
Answers will vary.

Page 18
Answers will vary.

Chapter 1 Post-Test

Page 19
Answers will vary.

Chapter 2

Lesson 1

Page 20
Answers will vary.

Page 21
Answers will vary.

Lesson 2

Page 22
Sentences will vary.

Page 23
Answers will vary.

Page 24
Answers will vary.

Lesson 3

Page 25
Answers will vary.

Page 26
first, next, last
next, last, first

Page 27
first, last, next
last, next, first

Lesson 4

Page 28
Sentences will vary.

Page 29
first, last, next
last, next, first
Sentences will vary.

Lesson 5

Page 30
Lists will vary.

Page 31
Lists will vary.

Lesson 6

Page 32
What kind of cloud is that?
Do you think it will rain?
When will the rain end?

Page 33
Questions will vary.

Page 34
what do pandas eat?
Where is the sun at night?
Questions will vary.

Chapter 2 Post-Test

Page 35
Answers will vary.
next, first, last

Answer Key

Chapter 3

Lesson 1
Page 37
Drawings will vary.

Page 38
Answers will vary.

Lesson 2
Page 40
Instructions will vary.

Page 41
Instructions will vary.

Lesson 3
Page 42
Lists will vary.

Page 43
Directions will vary.

Page 44
Directions will vary.

Lesson 4
Page 45
because   This happened

Page 46
There are two pieces of wood because it
    was chopped in half.
Pictures and sentences will vary.

Lesson 5
Page 47
Answers will vary.

Page 48
Answers will vary.

Page 49
Answers will vary.

Lesson 6
Page 50
Tina wrote this letter because her cousin is
    coming to visit.
Sentences will vary.

Page 52
Letters will vary.

Page 53
Letters will vary.

Chapter 3 Post-Test
Page 54
Answers will vary

Page 55
Letters will vary.

Answer Key

Chapter 4

Lesson 1

Page 56
Circled senses: seeing, smelling, touching, tasting
Circled senses: seeing, hearing, smelling, touching
Circled senses: seeing, smelling, touching

Page 57
Responses will vary.

Page 58
smell—skunk odor
hearing—water OR smell—fish, etc.
feeling—cold

Lesson 2

page 59
Responses will vary.

Page 60
Responses will vary.

Page 61
Responses will vary.

Lesson 3

Page 62
Answers to riddles: spaghetti, train, snake, log

Page 63
Riddles will vary.

Page 64
Riddles will vary.

Lesson 4

Page 65
Responses will vary.

Page 66
Responses will vary.

Page 67
Letters will vary.

Lesson 5

Page 68
These balloons are the same size.
These balloons are different colors.
These cars are the same color.
These cars are different sizes.
These horses are the same size.
These horses are different colors.

Page 69
Answers will vary.

Page 70
Answers will vary.

Lesson 6

Page 71
The first spider is bigger than the second.
The second spider is smaller than the first.
Dad is taller than Timmy.
Timmy is shorter than Dad.

Page 72
A bird is slower than a plane.
A plane is faster than a bird.
A car is faster than a bike.
A bike is slower than a car.
Sentences will vary.

Page 73
Sentences will vary.

Lesson 7

Page 75
Responses will vary.

Page 76
Responses will vary.

Lesson 8

Page 77
Responses will vary.

Chapter 4 continued

Page 78
Letters will vary.

Page 79
Letters will vary.

Chapter 4 Post-Test

Page 80
(dog) sight, sound, smell, touch
(food) sight, smell, touch, taste
Sentences will vary.

Page 81
Responses will vary.

Answer Key

Chapter 5

Lesson 1

Page 83
Characters: Dad, Sue
Beginning: Sue wonders what she and Dad will do.
Middle: Dad does many things. Sue watches.
End: Sue and Dad do something that they both can do.
rug: blue
windows: dirty
Other describing words will vary.

Lesson 2

Page 84
Sentences will vary.

Page 85
Sentences will vary.

Lesson 3

Page 86
Responses will vary.

Page 87
Responses will vary.

Page 88
Stories will vary.

Lesson 4

Page 89
Circled words or phrases: rain, played a game, get windy, bent back and forth, crack

Page 90
Responses will vary.

Page 91
Responses will vary.

Lesson 5

Page 92
Responses will vary.

Page 93
Responses will vary.

Page 94
Stories will vary.

Chapter 5 Post-Test

Page 95
Words in blanks: characters, fun, beginning, middle, end, describing
Responses will vary.

Page 96
Stories will vary.

Notes